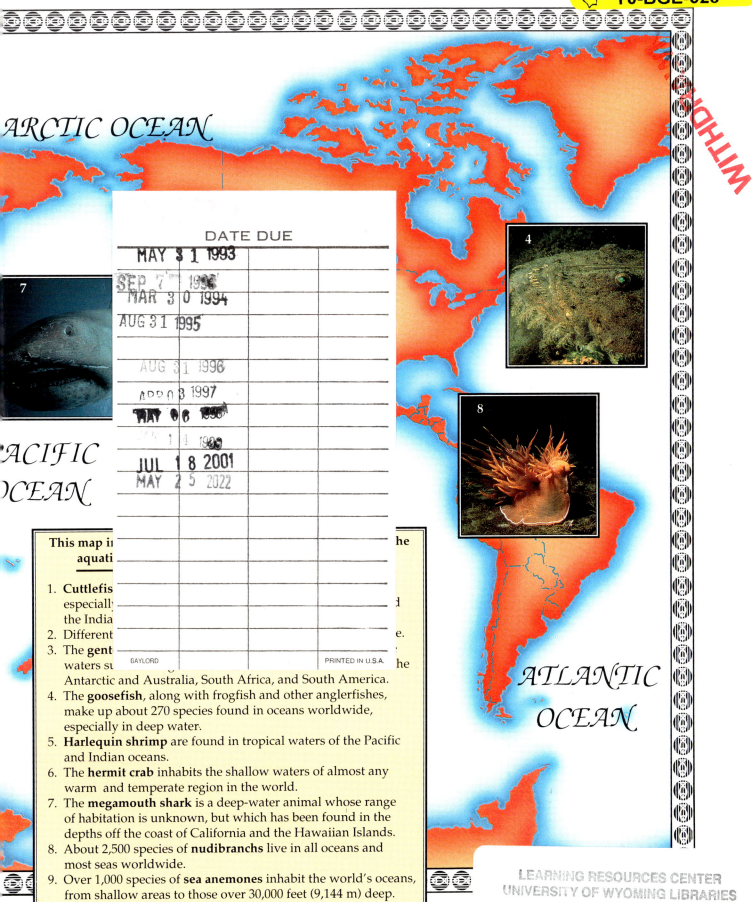

ARCTIC OCEAN

PACIFIC OCEAN

ATLANTIC OCEAN

4

8

7

This map in ... the aquati...

1. **Cuttlefis**... especially ... the India...
2. Different ...
3. The **gent**... waters su... he Antarctic and Australia, South Africa, and South America.
4. The **goosefish**, along with frogfish and other anglerfishes, make up about 270 species found in oceans worldwide, especially in deep water.
5. **Harlequin shrimp** are found in tropical waters of the Pacific and Indian oceans.
6. The **hermit crab** inhabits the shallow waters of almost any warm and temperate region in the world.
7. The **megamouth shark** is a deep-water animal whose range of habitation is unknown, but which has been found in the depths off the coast of California and the Hawaiian Islands.
8. About 2,500 species of **nudibranchs** live in all oceans and most seas worldwide.
9. Over 1,000 species of **sea anemones** inhabit the world's oceans, from shallow areas to those over 30,000 feet (9,144 m) deep.
10. **Whales** live in oceans and some rivers worldwide.

DON'T BLINK NOW!

CAPTURING THE HIDDEN WORLD OF SEA CREATURES

BY ANN DOWNER

A New England Aquarium Book

FRANKLIN WATTS

New York • London • Toronto • Sydney

1991

To Michael Bovino,
who likes most things
with feathers, fur, or fins
— A. D.

Acknowledgments

This book is based on the 1986 exhibit "Don't Blink Now!" at the New England Aquarium, Boston, Massachusetts, an exhibit that was made possible in part by the Shawmut National Corporation, on the occasion of its 150th anniversary, and by the Massachusetts Cultural Council, a state agency.

The author wishes to express her great appreciation to the staff of the New England Aquarium, including Les Kaufman, Alan Hankin, and especially Ken Mallory for his editorial guidance. Thanks also to Liz Gowell for her editorial review, and to Marcia Storkerson for her generous contribution of the gentoo penguin photographs taken in Antarctica.

Front cover collage: A giant orange sea slug attacks its favorite source of food—a tube-dwelling anemone.

Back cover: Having flipped a chocolate-chip sea star onto its back, a pair of harlequin shrimp prepare to devour their prey piecemeal.

Frontispiece collage: There are some kinds of anemones that cling to an anchoring surface so tightly it seems no force can pry them loose. The species of anemone shown here, on the other hand, is quick to release its grip on the surrounding rock so it can escape from its predator, a leather sea star.

World map illustrated by Joe Le Monnier
Diagram by Vantage Art, Inc.

Photographs copyright © : Fred Bavendam: pp. 1, 4, 6, 7, 9, 11, 14, 15, 20, 21, 23, 24, 28; New England Aquarium: pp. 12, 13 left, 17 (all Ken Mallory), 29 (Chris Newbert), 32 (Michael DeMocker); Animals Animals: pp. 13 top right (Scott Johnson), 13 bottom right (Carl Roessler); Andrew Martinez: p. 19; Marcia Storkerson: p. 27; Key Largo National Marine Sanctuary: pp. 30, 31; Bruce Elliott Rasner: pp. 34, 35.

Library of Congress Cataloging-in-Publication Data

Downer, Ann, 1960–
    Don't blink now! : capturing the hidden world of sea creatures / by Ann Downer ; [diagrams by James Needham].
        p.   cm.
        "A New England Aquarium book."
        Includes bibliographical references and index.
        Summary: Underwater photographs capture marine animals in the acts of birth, growth, the hunt, and death.
        ISBN 0-531-15225-1.
        ISBN 0-531-11072-9 (lib. bdg.)
        1. Marine fauna—Juvenile literature. [1. Marine animals.] I. Needham, James, ill. II. Title.
    QL 122.2.D69 1991
    591.92—dc20   91-18733 CIP AC

C O N T E N T S

Fishes such as this sculpin from the Pacific coast of Canada have good reason to hang around in the ocean mud. Buried up to its eyes, the sculpin can make a swift meal of unsuspecting prey.

ENTER A SECRET WORLD

In the world of the ocean, the quick, the hidden, and the well-protected survive. Animals with the advantage of speed are better able to hunt and escape from other hunters. Some animals move slowly or not at all. In order to survive, they have to outwit their prey and enemies using camouflage, armor, or built-in poisons or venoms.

And that's the whole problem with trying to observe life under water. Many of the creatures that live there move so fast—or so slowly—that it is hard to catch them in the act of hunting, escaping, or reproducing.

Unlike an action-packed movie, events in nature unfold in bits and pieces. Sudden and dramatic action is followed by long periods of stillness and silence. Walk into a rain forest and you may sit for hours before seeing the slightest movement of a butterfly or tree-snake. Or look through a glass-bottomed boat at a coral reef. You may see a school of brightly colored fish dart past, but the real action is lost in movements so quick and secret they are rarely seen.

Scientists and underwater photographers have learned how to capture these rare moments on film. By freezing a split second in time or condensing the events that sometimes take place over hours into a few pages or photographs, this book gives you a front-row seat at the life-and-death dramas of a fascinating and beautiful world.

Through underwater photography from around the globe, *Don't Blink Now!* catches marine animals as they pass through the drama and pageantry of birth, growth, the hunt—and being hunted—and, inevitably, death.

From the deep, cold waters of British Columbia, Canada, to the Great Barrier Reef off the coast of Australia to the frozen terrain of Antarctica, you will get closer than you ever dreamed possible to some of the most interesting animals that inhabit the sea.

(Right) A cockleshell knows what to do
when it encounters a hungry scavenger
such as the moon snail. The cockleshell
uses its muscular foot to catapult
itself out of danger.

CHAPTER ONE

AN EAT-OR-BE-EATEN WORLD

Some predators chase down their prey. Some stay put and lay a trap instead. And some predators only have to open their mouths: The giant, gentle manta ray swims with its mouth wide open and lets its lunch of plankton and krill float right in.

But, for most animals that live in the sea, finding a meal isn't always that easy. To find food, every predator has inherited—or evolved—special attributes: a streamlined shape, a clever disguise, or a venomous sting. Let's look at some of the ways a hungry hunter gets enough to eat in the eat-or-be-eaten underwater world.

DINER, BEWARE!

Suppose you took a fish and squashed it almost flat, so that it looked like a frying pan with fins and a tail? Well, you might end up with something like the goosefish.

This diver off the coast of Maine is holding a goosefish gently by its pectoral fins. Unlike the more familiar flounder, this flat fish is almost all mouth. But despite its array of teeth, the diver isn't in any danger. Smaller fishes, however, are another matter!

It's hard to tell where the goosefish ends and the ocean floor begins: Its sides are fringed with flaps of skin that look like seaweed, and its bumpy, warty top blends in with the gravelly bottom.

The goosefish spends much of its time half-buried on the ocean floor. Since it isn't fast enough to chase its prey, the goosefish must attract fish to bring them within catching range. It does this with a lure attached to the end of its long spine, which it can move in any direction, like a worm on the end of a fishing pole. Once a fish swims close enough, the goosefish wiggles the lure in front of its own mouth and. . .

. . .WHOOSH! The goosefish suddenly opens its mouth and the smaller fish is swept inside. Needle-sharp teeth fold back on hinges to let the prey in, then snap back into place to keep the fish from swimming out again. Those curved teeth are not made for chewing; the goosefish swallows its meal whole. The slits on the bottom of its mouth are gills. They're smaller than the gills belonging to most fish its size. This is because its ambush method of hunting is so efficient. The goosefish hardly moves, so it doesn't need to get as much oxygen from the water.

FANTASTIC FINS

The goosefish's lure is a specially adapted dorsal, or back, fin. Fins are often adapted in amazing ways, enabling fish to lure prey, escape predators, attract a mate, "fly" above the water, or even—in the case of walking catfish—cross a highway! Fins can be venomous weapons, as seen with the scorpionfish, or fancy camouflage. The sargassum fish has fins that are elaborately adapted to make it blend in with the sargassum weed in which the fish makes its home.

(Facing page, left) A diver poses with the goosefish, Lophius americanus, raised above his head. (Right) The goosefish takes the game of fishing quite seriously. A special spine on its back lures a potential meal in close, and faster than this camera was able to capture, the goosefish inhales its prey.

LIONESS
OF THE DEEP

If you think only a big fish can be a predator, think again. Meet one of the most successful hunters of the sea: sneaky, determined, bright orange, and only 6 inches (15.2 cm) long! No, this isn't an alien life-form from a monster movie. It's a nudibranch, or sea slug—a distant relative of garden slugs.

Not only do animals have to outwit their prey—they also have to outwit other predators vying with them for the same meal. One way to beat the competition is to eat something no one else can swallow.

The giant nudibranch shown here has developed a knack for eating a particularly unappetizing food—the stinging tentacles of the sea anemone. Rearing up, the nudibranch lunges at the anemone and bites off some of its tentacles. After coating them with a special mucus, the nudibranch can swallow the tentacles without injuring itself. Some kinds of nudibranchs (not the one shown here) take the anemone's barbed stinging cells and transfer them to the fingerlike stalks that extend from the nudibranch's back, where they work in much the same way as they did on the anemone. Besides gaining a meal, such nudibranchs have acquired a new means of protecting themselves.

Believe it or not, the anenome sometimes survives the attack, and the tentacles it has lost grow back to provide lunch for another nudibranch someday.

AND HE TASTES BAD, TOO

The nudibranch should be easy prey: It is small, it has no shell, and its bright colors make it hard to miss. But this small predator can defend itself in several ways. The same bright colors that make it easy to spot also flash the warning message "Don't touch!" Many nudibranchs taste terrible to other fish. Any predator that swallows them spits them right out again. Ptui! Other nudibranchs successfully recycle the stinging cells from the anemones they eat.

(Facing page) An orange sea slug pounces on its favorite source of food, a tube-dwelling anemone. Even the anemone's stinging cells don't discourage this hungry predator.

DINNER FOR TWO

Harlequin shrimp make their burrows in the coral reef, coming out at night to stalk their favorite food—sea stars. These rare shrimp mate for life, perhaps because they have so few mates (and valuable hunting partners) from which to choose. Alone, a single harlequin is no match for a sea star, but two shrimp working together can overturn a spiny prey.

Scientists disagree about the actual method harlequin shrimp use to flip the sea star over. Some believe the shrimp first use their front claws to nip off the sea star's tiny suction feet. Others say the sea star draws its feet back as a protective reflex. Either way, the sea star loses its grip, and the shrimp can peel one arm off the surface of the rock. Then, using the sea star's arm as a lever, the harlequin shrimp flip the sea star onto its back, sort of like a judo throw. Once on its back, the sea star is defenseless. After dragging it back to their burrow, the couple devour their prey, taking up to two weeks to polish it off, one arm at a time.

(Right) A pair of harlequin shrimp gang up on a chocolate-chip sea star. First they isolate one of the sea star's arms to pry it free from a rock. Then the two shrimp roll the sea star over, exposing its unprotected belly.

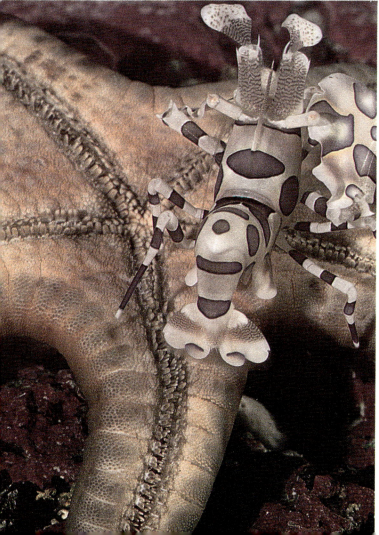

A THORNY PROBLEM

One of the harlequin shrimp's favorite foods is the crown-of-thorns sea star. The crown-of-thorns is a well-known culprit responsible for widespread damage to the coral reefs. The sea stars eat coral by turning their stomachs inside out, then smothering and digesting the small animals that live inside the rock-like coral formation. Enough hungry sea stars can do a lot of damage, but scientists now think that invasions of this damaging sea star may be regular events and that the crown-of-thorns poses much less threat to reefs than we humans do.

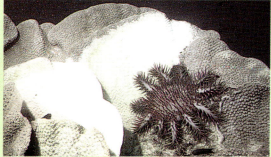

(Top) The crown-of-thorns sea star was once thought to be the coral reef's worst natural predator. (Bottom) This sea star lies on a bed of corals whose polyps it has devoured, leaving behind a trail of bleached coral skeleton.

(Left and facing page) Two sun stars off Canada's Pacific coast literally link arms in an underwater version of Star Wars. The smaller star may have been trying to pull food away from its larger opponent.

CHAPTER TWO

THE GREAT SURVIVAL GAME

We've seen some of the special ways predators hunt and trap their dinners. But what if *you're* the dinner? Suppose you're the prey instead of the predator? You'd better have some way to protect yourself, to outwit, confuse, frighten, or disgust your enemy: a shell too tough to crack, a confusing color pattern, a scary mask, or a terrible taste.

One of the oldest and most effective forms of protection is the shell. But what if you weren't born with a built-in suit of underwater armor?

If you're a hermit crab, you go out and find one.

WANTED:
Used Mobile Home in Good Condition

The hermit crab, a member of the group of animals scientists call crustaceans, is as closely related to lobsters as it is to other crabs. Its scientific name, "anomurans," means "odd-tailed," which refers in the hermit crab's case to its soft hind end, which curves most often to the right. This odd tail allows the hermit to quickly back into the spiral shell that was vacated by a snail. The blown-glass "shell" here shows the grippers at the end of the tail that help to make up for an otherwise loose fit.

Using secondhand shells is not without its drawbacks. For instance, the shell can't continue to grow as the crab does. Before long, the hermit crab will need a bigger "home."

Changing shells is a dangerous business. Leaving the safety of the shell for even a moment could mean being snapped up by a predator. After spotting an empty shell, the hermit crab first must make sure it *is* empty. It uses its claws to feel for holes, stones—or a current occupant! Once satisfied that the shell is safe and in good shape, the hermit may "try it on for size" several times—in much the same way you might test out a pair of shoes in a store to make sure they fit before you buy.

"Used" shells are hard to come by, and hermit crabs are known to fight over a particularly choice find. That's when a good fit really matters. If the hermit's new home is too roomy, a rival might be able to dislodge the new occupant and move itself in. A shell that's too tight, however, makes the hermit aggressive and more likely to start a fight over a shell.

HAVE SHELL, WILL TRAVEL

The hermit crab's ancestors were shell-less animals that hid in crevices in the coral reef to protect their soft bodies. Somewhere along the evolutionary trail, the first hermit crab used an abandoned snail shell for a home. This was a big improvement over living in a burrow, for one important reason. The hermit crab's ancestors had to leave the safety of the shelter in order to find food. With a shell, the hermit never has to leave home. Wherever it goes, the hermit crab carries its safe retreat on its back.

(Facing page) A hermit crab does not make its decision to change into a more suitable shell without first carefully probing inside its new potential home. After all, another animal could already be hiding in there.

THIS CRAB
TAKES EIGHT HOURS
TO GET DRESSED

Having a shell is one way animals protect themselves. Camouflage is another.

Most animals that use camouflage to protect themselves are born with their protective color patterns. Others can change color to blend in with their background, whether it is the gravelly gray ocean bottom or a bright red coral or sponge.

Then there are some animals that have developed behaviors to make up for the protective coloring nature never gave them. Meet the decorator crab.

The top of the decorator crab's shell is covered with tiny hooks, much like one-half of a Velcro fastener. To begin decorating, the crab gathers seaweed and debris from the ocean floor with its front claws. Nibbling the edges to roughen them, the crab then drags each piece of plant or animal material across its back until it catches on one of the tiny hooks. When its shell has been completely covered in this fashion, the crab decorates its front claws. As the crab grows, it molts, shedding its old shell for a larger one. Each new shell has to be decorated, which can take up to eight hours' work. One species of decorator crab even decorates its front claws with small sea anemones, which it then uses as weapons.

(Facing page) The decorator crab is In constant search for new bits of underwater debris. Decked out on its back and all around its body, such collected trash helps to hide its crab host from hungry predators.

BEATING A HASTY RETREAT

Most sea anemones spend their lives "rooted" to the ocean floor. (Since anemones are animals and not plants, they don't really have roots, but they do fasten themselves to one spot by means of a suction disk.) Using a twitching, pulsing motion, anemones can move around after a fashion. This enables them to take advantage of more sources of food than if they were locked into one spot.

Sometimes, however, an anemone's awkward "swimming" style serves a more important purpose. Take this anemone (see right), for instance. It has just made the unpleasant discovery that it has landed on a leather star. A large sea star that is one of the anemone's natural enemies, the leather star would have had a tasty meal if the anemone hadn't beat a hasty retreat.

(Right) Due to the absence of algae under this dislodged anemone, you can see it was probably perched there for quite some time. A suction disk at the anemone's base holds the anemone securely in place—until its natural enemy, the leather star, decides to come around.

IN THE BLINK
OF AN EYE

The cuttlefish is smaller than its relative, the octopus, and has ten tentacles instead of eight. When danger threatens, both animals can release a cloud of ink from a special sac, which allows them to escape while it distracts their enemies.

Ink is only one way the cuttlefish protects itself from its predators. It can also use a variety of color changes and patterns to confuse would-be attackers. No, the cuttlefish isn't blushing; it is actually shrinking and expanding pigment cells in order to change color (see diagram on page 23). The brain sends a message through its nervous system, which in turn expands or contracts muscle fibers in the pigment cells. It's as though you could make freckles appear and disappear to confuse your enemies.

Cuttlefish can summon a variety of patterns to their rescue. Two large dark circles, called eyespots, can fool a predator into thinking the cuttlefish is a larger and more threatening animal. A pattern of zebra stripes makes the cuttlefish hard to see when it is swimming. A pattern of uneven spots makes it difficult to spot against the sand. The cuttlefish can even change from light to dark in the blink of an eye, so its predator suddenly can't figure out where its prey has disappeared to.

Why does it need so many patterns to protect itself? Scientists think they're designed to fool especially smart predators. Some predators may have learned through experience that the cuttlefish's big eyespots are just a trick. So nature has given the cuttlefish several other disguises—stripes, and, when all else fails, there's always ink.

(Facing page) It's hard to imagine that the cuttlefish shown in these two photos is the same animal photographed only seconds apart. By expanding and contracting its color pigment cells—under control of the animal's nervous system—the cuttlefish can change its appearance almost instantaneously.

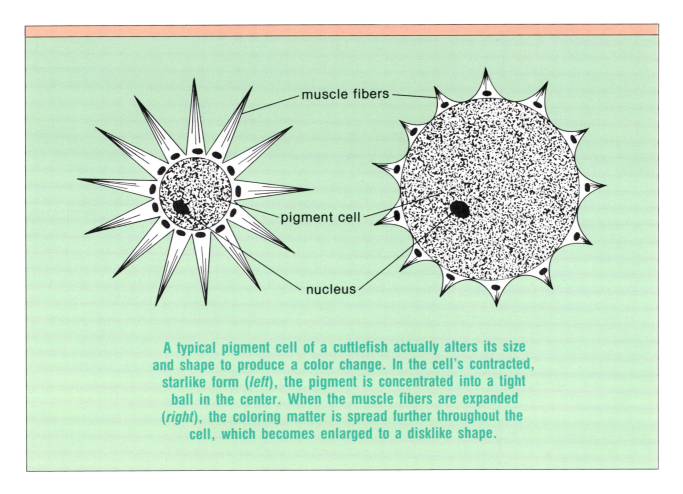

muscle fibers

pigment cell

nucleus

A typical pigment cell of a cuttlefish actually alters its size and shape to produce a color change. In the cell's contracted, starlike form (*left*), the pigment is concentrated into a tight ball in the center. When the muscle fibers are expanded (*right*), the coloring matter is spread further throughout the cell, which becomes enlarged to a disklike shape.

CHAPTER THREE

REPRODUCTION: THE ULTIMATE SURVIVAL SKILL

Hunting and self-defense skills help a single animal survive. A successful hunter or escape artist will live to hunt or escape another day. But the ultimate survival skill in nature is reproducing—passing a set of genetic codes on to the next generation. This ensures the whole species will survive, not just one individual.

For some marine animals, reproducing is as simple as splitting themselves in two. An anemone, for instance, reproduces by budding. A small anemone grows out of the side of the parent and eventually splits off. At the other end of the spectrum is the blue whale, the largest animal ever to live on the face of the earth. After a pregnancy lasting eleven months, the mother whale gives birth to a baby weighing two tons!

Most marine animals do little in the way of parenting except to lay their eggs in a protected place, and lay them in such large numbers that at least some are likely to survive. But some marine animals protect and feed their young after birth, sometimes even in the most extreme conditions.

(Facing page) A colony of staghorn coral releases bundles of eggs and sperm during an annual mass coral spawning on Australia's Great Barrier Reef. The union of sperm and egg results in a larva called a planula, which then settles on the reef floor.

PARENTING, PENGUIN-STYLE

Antarctica doesn't seem like a very good place to raise one's young. At the height of the Antarctic summer, the daytime temperature rarely climbs above freezing. As cold and forbidding as it may seem, it suits the gentoo penguin just fine. Oddly enough, with their dense, furlike feathers and thick layer of fat, penguins sometimes have to take a swim to keep cool.

Gentoos live on the Antarctic peninsula closest to the tip of South America and in the Falkland Islands. Unlike other species of penguins, gentoos don't fast before courtship, but take turns fishing and building their nest.

During the nesting season, gentoos carry rocks along trails to penguin community nurseries, where they build nests. While the eggs are incubating, the gentoo parents take twenty-four-hour shifts sitting on the eggs to keep them warm. Once the young have hatched, one parent relieves the other every twelve hours.

Look closely: This gentoo (see photo on facing page, far right) doesn't have a pot-belly. That flap of skin near its feet is a brood patch, an opening in the penguin's stomach feathers, where babies can hide and keep warm. Peeking out from underneath is a baby gentoo.

BETWEEN A ROCK AND A HARD PLACE

A penguin's nest may not seem practical at first glance. Yet the penguin's nest works perfectly well for the penguin. How can a cone-shaped pile of stones on the cold ground work as well as a feather-lined nest high in the branches of a tree? The penguin builds its nest out of rocks because they are the only nesting material available in the frozen Antarctic. The heap of stones, though simple, serves several important functions. It keeps the egg up off the frozen ground, thus helping to keep it warm. It holds the egg high enough off the ground so that it won't be washed away by the occasional thaw. And last, but not least, the nest keeps the precious egg from rolling down a slope of ground.

(Facing page) Gentoo penguin feathers allow the adult penguin to be well-equipped to survive in its icy Antarctic home. But baby gentoos need a little extra help to combat the cold. The stomach brood pouch of the parent allows the youngster to snuggle close to the skin of the nurturing adult for warmth.

A REEF IS BORN

It is summer in Australia, and under a December moon at the Great Barrier Reef something extraordinary is happening. The water is teeming with tiny white creatures, each no bigger than a kernel of corn. These are the fertilized eggs of the staghorn coral. It's hard to believe that something so small can eventually build a limestone reef 500 feet (152 m) thick, a structure strong enough to resist crashing ocean surf.

For a few days, the coral larva, called a planula, floats in the warm sea. This is a dangerous time for the planula: Most of the millions of fertilized coral eggs released into the ocean are eaten by fish and other predators. Using tiny oarlike hairs to propel itself through the water, the growing planula swims to a safe spot.

There the planula flattens itself out and begins to cement itself to the rocky bottom with a sticky fluid that hardens into a limestone skeleton. After four weeks, the coral's tentacles have formed. The planula is now a mature coral animal, called a polyp. Now the coral is surrounded by a limestone cup that looks like one section of an upside-down egg carton. Inside this stony outer skeleton lives the polyp itself: six tentacles that pass food to a mouth in the center.

From this mass of tiny fertilized eggs result millions of coral animals that help build the coral reef. The coral colony produces eggs in enormous quantity because most never survive long enough to reach maturity. They are swept up as food by hungry dwellers of the coral reef.

THE BIGGEST, LITTLEST ARCHITECTS

Corals are really colonies of many polyps that have fused together. As a coral colony grows, it secretes limestone, building new skeletons on top of the old ones, and "gluing" in shells and rocks. In this way, corals have formed reefs more than 1,000 miles (1,609.3 km) long. Next to us, coral is the animal species that has done the most to change the surface of the earth.

(Facing page) Coral colonies assume myriad shapes, including the myriad furrows of the brain. Each colony consists of thousands of tiny coral polyps which help the reef grow.

DEATH COMES TO THE CORAL REEF

These dramatic before-and-after photographs show the death of a coral reef. The coral polyps die, leaving a bleached white skeleton. Waters that were once clear and teeming with marine life are now murky with algae, the only form of life they can now support.

These photographs show a reef off the coast of Florida, but scientists have found damage to reefs all over the world. What is killing the coral reefs? Scientists originally blamed the crown-of-thorns, a sea star that preys on coral. But the damage is too widespread to be caused by the crown-of-thorns alone. The more likely culprit is human beings.

In our desire to study and play in this spectacular underwater habitat, we have been, literally, smothering the coral reef with attention. When hotels and resorts are built near coral reefs, eroded soil and human waste are washed into the lagoon. If the silt itself doesn't block the sunlight necessary for coral growth, the sewage allows algae to grow out of control and compete for precious oxygen necessary for corals to breathe.

As is true of rain forests, coral reefs are home to many animals that may become extinct before scientists have time to even give them names. The reefs need to be pre-

served, not only for their beauty but for the many things scientists still have to learn about the animals that live there.

These photographs contrast a healthy elkhorn coral site (below) with one on the facing page that shows how boat anchor dragging can damage a reef. Hurricanes, pollution from industrial runoff, and increasing temperatures resulting from global climate change are thought to be other agents of destruction.

A Jump For Joy? The humpback whale is one of the true acrobats of the sea. In a behavior called breaching, the humpback lifts all 30 to 50 tons of its weight completely out of the water, then falls back with an enormous splash into the sea. No one really knows why whales breach. Scientists have variously offered theories that perhaps it is a form of underwater communication between whales during bad weather, a display of courtship, an attempt to dislodge stubborn parasites, or simply just plain fun. For the time being, breaching is one of the many mysteries of the ocean that is yet to be resolved.

THE FUTURE

Otto Elliott, a commercial fisherman in California, recently pulled a strange fish out of the deep waters 7 miles (about 11.72 km) offshore from Dana Point Harbor in Los Angeles, California. Elliot suspected he had caught something unusual. This fish had luminous organs inside its huge mouth. Standing in a phone booth, he called museum after museum to tell scientists about his discovery. Finally, he reached Bob Lavenberg, curator of fishes at the Los Angeles County Museum of Natural History, and described the fish he had found. It was 15 feet (about 4.5m) long and looked like a baby killer whale. Excited, the scientist sped to the site and found that the fisherman had pulled a live megamouth from the ocean.

Only five other megamouths had ever been found before; none had survived. But the megamouth lives at such extreme depths that no aquarium was equipped to take it. In a race against time, Lavenberg measured, photographed, and then attached radio transmitters to the creature so he could track its movement. Then he and the fisherman released it back to the sea.

New submersibles—small robot submarines outfitted to collect data from the furthest depths of the ocean—are opening up a new frontier, a world as alien to human life as the far reaches of the galaxy. Young people reading this book will grow up and possibly become the next generation of scientists. Perhaps they will travel to the dark home of the mysterious megamouth or learn the secret of why humpback whales breach. A few of them may discover new forms of life never seen before by anyone.

Maybe one of those scientists will be you.

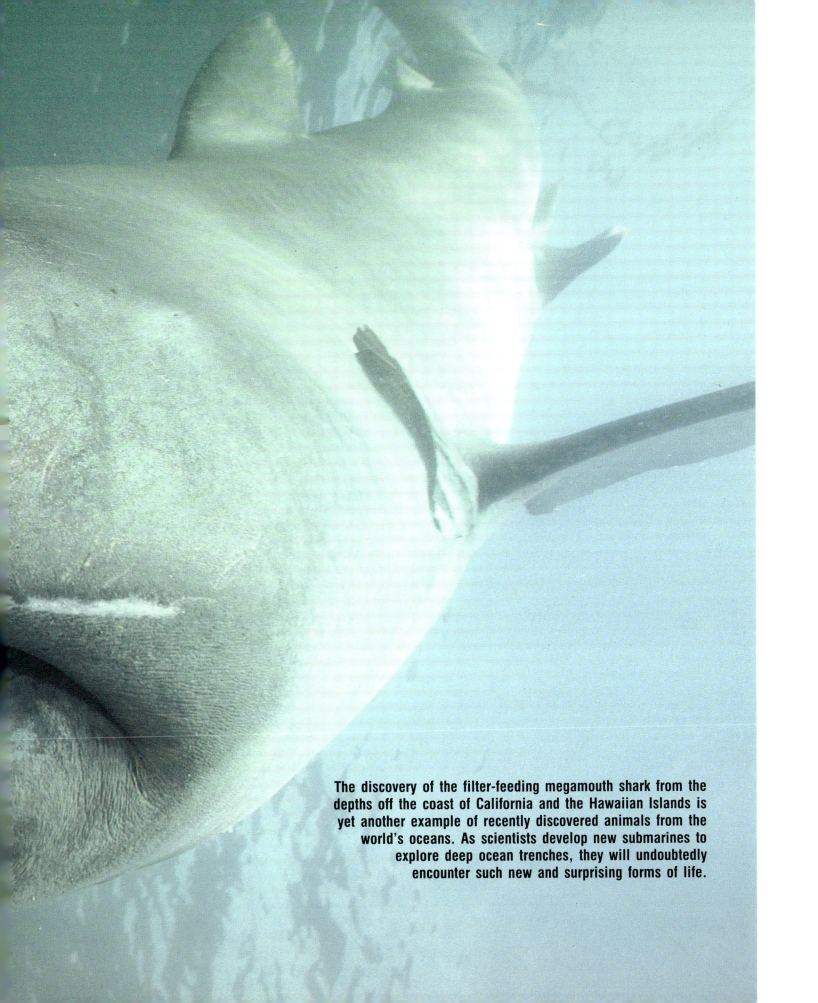

The discovery of the filter-feeding megamouth shark from the depths off the coast of California and the Hawaiian Islands is yet another example of recently discovered animals from the world's oceans. As scientists develop new submarines to explore deep ocean trenches, they will undoubtedly encounter such new and surprising forms of life.

GLOSSARY

Breach (BREECH)—An acrobatic leaping behavior of some whales and even some sharks that allows them to jump sometimes completely out of water before falling back again, usually with a huge splash.

Brood patch—A bare area of skin on a bird's belly used for keeping eggs warm and protected.

Budding—A method of reproduction in which an animal splits off part of its cell material to produce another animal instead of uniting sperm and eggs.

Camouflage (KAM-uh-flazh)—To hide or disguise oneself by blending body color or shape into the background.

Coral reef (KOR-ul REEF)—A huge natural formation made by the limestone skeletons of coral animals found only in the tropics.

Crustaceans (kru-STAY-shuns)—Invertebrate animals—such as shrimp, crabs, lobsters, and barnacles—with a hard outer shell and jointed appendages.

Dorsal fin (DOR-sul FIN)—Fin located on or near the back of an animal.

Gills (GILS)—Feathery organs on both sides of the head or body of fishes and aquatic invertebrates that absorb oxygen from water and remove carbon dioxide from the blood.

Incubate (IN-kyuh-bate)—To keep eggs warm so they will hatch.

Krill (KRIL)—Small shrimplike saltwater animals that are the main food source of many baleen whales, including the blue whale.

Leather star—A sea star from the Pacific coast of North America that feeds on sea anemones, sea cucumbers, sea urchins, and a variety of other invertebrates.

Megamouth (MEY-guh-MOUTH)—A kind of deepwater shark with a huge cavernous mouth equipped with bioluminescent organs, apparently to attract prey.

Mucus (MYOO-kus)—A thick, slimy substance made by the body of an animal to help it do something, such as digest food.

Nudibranch (NOO-duh-brank)—A marine animal related to snails but unlike the snail, the nudibranch only has a shell during its larval stage.

Pectoral fin (PEK-tor-ul FIN)—One of a pair of fins usually located on the sides of a fish's body behind the gill covers.

Photosynthesis (FOE-toe-SIN-tuh-sis)—Process by which plants convert the sun, carbon dioxide, and water into energy in the form of sugars, starches, and other foods.

Pigment cells—Cells that produce reflective or absorbing materials and therefore color in plants and animals, especially important in vision.

Planula (PLAN-yuh-luh)—The free-swimming early life-form of sea anemones, corals, jellyfishes, and their relatives.

Polyp (POL-up)—A stage in the lives of jellyfishes, sea anemones, and corals consisting of a simple stomach with a mouth surrounded by tentacles.

Poison —A substance which must be eaten or swallowed to kill or injure its victim. Venom, on the other hand, must be injected by fangs, spines, or stinging cells.

Predators (PRED-uh-turz)—Animals that eat other animals.

Sargassum fish (sar-GAS-um FISH)—A small fish, up to 6 inches (15.2 cm) long, that hides among the floating sargassum weed of the Sargasso Sea, a huge body of warm sea water currents in the North Atlantic. The sargassum fish is an anglerfish; it attracts food to a lure near its mouth. The lure is a specially adapted ray of one of the sargassum fish's fins.

Sea anemone (SEE uh-NEM-uh-nee) —A single polyp that resembles a flower and is a relative of jellyfishes and corals. An anemone consists of a simple stomach with a mouth surrounded by tentacles.

Tentacles (TEN-tuh-kuls)—Long, flexible structures usually on an animal's head or around its mouth, used for grasping or stinging.

Venom (VEH-num)—Unlike poison, which must be eaten or swallowed to affect its victim, venom is a harmful substance which must be injected by fangs, spines, or stinging cells.

BIBLIOGRAPHY

Books and References:

Banister, Keith, and Andrew Campbell. *The Illustrated Encyclopedia of Aquatic Life* (New York: Facts on File, 1985). An encyclopedia with color photos that reviews watery environments from rivers, ponds, and lakes to oceans and seas. Information drawn from this book includes pp. 90–7 on anglerfishes; 172–81 on sea anemones, jellyfishes, and corals; 234–40 on hermit crabs; 274–83 on spiny creatures such as sea stars; and 290–340 on whales and dolphins.

Barnes, Robert D. *Invertebrate Zoology* 5th edition (Philadelphia, London, Toronto: W. B. Saunders Company, 1987). This authoritative textbook (not light reading) is the last word in learning about invertebrates, for understanding both their classification and behaviors.

Cousteau, J., and staff of the Cousteau Society. *The Cousteau Almanac* (New York: Doubleday & Company, 1981). An imaginative look at the ocean world, and a model for many of the latest books reviewing the promise (in the form of minerals, medicines, tidal power, and the harvest of food) and the problems facing the water planet.

Curtis, B. *The Life Story of the Fish: His Manners and Morals* (New York: Dover Publications, 1961). A classic presentation of the story of fishes which, even thirty years later, is rich with clear and useful information.

Durrell, Lee. *State of the Ark* (New York: Doubleday & Company, 1986). A review of the environmental issues facing us worldwide, some of the leading trouble spots, and what we can do to manage them.

Edmunds, E. *Defense in Animals* (Essex, England: Longman, 1974). An advanced book (not for children) which explains some of our understanding of animal behavior, including land and water animals. Cuttlefish discussion on pp. 15, 29–30, 165–6, 170, 175; nudibranchs 37, 236–8.

Gosner, Kenneth. *A Field Guide to the Atlantic Seashore,* The Peterson Guide Series (Boston: Houghton Mifflin, 1978). Field guide information to animals and plants of the Atlantic seashore, which includes descriptions of hermit crabs, decorator crabs, and other animals described in *Don't Blink Now!*

Harrison, Sir Richard, and M. M. Bryden. *Whales, Dolphins, and Porpoises* (New York: Facts on File, 1988). Lucid, comprehensive, and readable look at the world of water mammals which includes some of the most recent research findings, illustrated with color photos and other artwork.

Herald, Earl. *Fishes of North America* (New York: Doubleday & Company, 1972). This is the fish counterpart of the Lorus and Margery Milne book, *Invertebrates of North America.*

Jacobson, M., and D. Franz. *Wonders of Corals and Coral Reefs* (New York: Dodd, Mead & Company, 1979). A children's book that is also useful for the adult and the older child in understanding how reefs that are thousands of miles long are built by creatures the size of a pencil eraser.

_____*Wonders of Snails and Slugs* (New York: Dodd, Mead & Company, 1980). A children's book about snails and sea slugs told with authority and skill, useful for the adult and the older child in understanding how animals that seem so unprotected have adapted to live in the sea.

Kaplan, E. *A Field Guide to Coral Reefs of the Caribbean and Florida* (Boston: Houghton Mifflin, 1982). A field guide to identify and understand the various interrelationships on a coral reef, with color and black-and-white photos.

Levine, J. *Undersea Life* (New York: Stewart, Tabori & Chang, 1985). A beautifully illustrated book with color photos, told by a marine scientist and conservationist, with a clear look at the evolution of ocean life, its habitats, and the interdependence of its many forms of life.

Mash, Kaye. *How Invertebrates Live* (London: Elsevier-Phaidon, 1975). A close-up presentation that includes how invertebrates adapt to their environments, find food, reproduce, and protect themselves, as well as information on cuttlefish, sea stars, nudibranchs, sea anemones, corals, and crabs.

Milne, Lorus and Margery. *Invertebrates of North America* (New York: Doubleday & Company, 1972). An adult book that reviews the different kinds of invertebrates, their classifications, and behaviors.

Robins, Richard C., G. Carleton Ray, and John Douglass. *Atlantic Coast Fishes of North America,* Peterson Field Guides (Boston: Houghton Mifflin, 1986). Field guide for identifying the various fishes on the Eastern Seaboard as well as those referred to in *Don't Blink Now!*

Simpson, G. *Penguins: Past and Present, Here and There* (New Haven and London: Yale University Press, 1976). An adult book that includes discussion of the evolution of penguins, their life histories, and the impact of commercial hunting.

Thompson, T. E. *Nudibranchs* (Neptune City, New Jersey: TFH Publications, 1976). One of the most wide-ranging reviews of nudibranchs available, which includes where they live, how they live, and how they are related to other invertebrates.

Todd, Frank S. *The Sea World Book of Penguins*, A Sea World Book for Young Readers (New York and London: Harcourt Brace Jovanovich, 1981). A children's book that includes a discussion of gentoo penguins and some seventeen other varieties.

Whitfield, Philip. *The Hunters*. (New York: Simon and Schuster, 1978). Illustrated book that reviews strategies of predators and prey across the animal kingdom from land to sea. Crown-of-thorns sea star discussion on pp. 106–7, anglerfish (goosefish), 46–7, sea anemone 100–1, section on prey defenses 142–7.

Magazine Articles and Periodicals:

"Antarctica's Well-Bred Penguins." Susan G. Trivelpiece and Wayne Z. Trivelpiece, *Natural History*, December 1989.

"Corals and Coral Reefs," Thomas F. Goreau, Nora I. Goreau, and Thomas J. Goreau, *Scientific American*, August 1979.

"Life Cycle of a Coral," Robert F. Sisson, *National Geographic*, June 1973.

FOR FURTHER READING

Banister, Keith, and Andrew Campbell. *The Illustrated Encyclopedia of Aquatic Life*. New York: Facts on File, 1985.

Bunting, Eve. *The Sea World Book of Whales*, A Sea World Book for Young Readers. New York and London: Harcourt Brace Jovanovich, 1980.

Jacobson, Morris, and David Franz. *Wonders of Corals and Coral Reefs*. Dodd, Mead & Company, 1979.

_____*Wonders of Snails & Slugs*. Dodd, Mead & Company, 1980.

Jacobson, Morris and William K. Emerson. *Wonders of Starfish*. Dodd, Mead & Company, 1977.

Mash, Kaye. *How Invertebrates Live*. London: Elsevier-Phaidon, 1975.

Milne, Margery. *Invertebrates of North America*. New York: Doubleday and Company, 1972.

Parker, Steve. *Fish: Eyewitness Books*. New York: Alfred A. Knopf, 1990.

Patent, Dorothy Hinshaw. *Fish and How They Reproduce*. New York: Holiday House, 1976.

Ranger Rick. *Amazing Creatures of the Sea*. Washington: National Wildlife Federation, 1987.

_____*Endangered Animals*. Washington: National Wildlife Federation, 1989.

Todd, Frank S. *The Sea World Book of Penguins*, A Sea World Book for Young Readers. New York and London: Harcourt Brace Jovanovich, 1981.

Whitfield, Philip. *The Hunters*. New York: Simon and Schuster, 1978.

INDEX

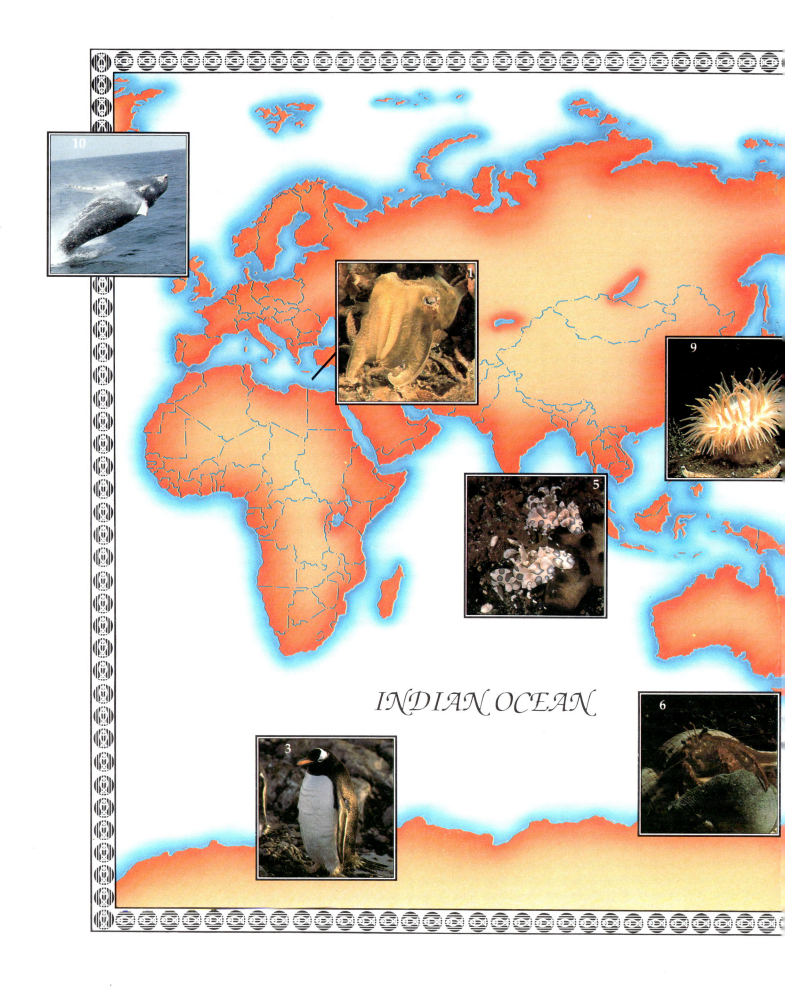

INDIAN OCEAN